Company's Coming

150 DELICIOUS SQUARES

SAUTÉED CABBAGE

An economical vegetable. It has a very faint hint of sauerkraut flavor.

Chopped or sliced onion	¾ cup	175 mL
Water		
Grated cabbage, packed	4 cups	900 mL
Vegetable cooking oil	1 tbsp.	15 mL
Vinegar	1 tbsp.	15 mL

Combine onion and water in frying pan. Cover. Simmer until soft.

Add cabbage. Stir. Add more water if needed. Cover. Simmer about 6 minutes until cabbage is tender crisp.

Add cooking oil and vinegar. Stir-fry about 20 to 25 minutes until sautéed and water has boiled away. Makes 2 cups (450 mL).

¼ cup125 mL contains:

Energy		61 Calories (254 kJ)
Cholesterol		0 mg
Sodium		14 mg
Fat		4 g

Taste the Tradition

Company's Coming

PINT SIZE BOOKS

By Jean Paré

BEVERAGES

Copyright ©1997 by Company's Coming Publishing Limited
All Rights Reserved

Second Printing October 1997

ISBN 1-895455-31-6

Published and Distributed by
Company's Coming Publishing Limited
Box 8037, Station "F"
Edmonton, Alberta, Canada
T6H 4N9

**Published Simultaneously in
Canada and the United States of America**

Front and Back Cover Photo

1. Caesar, page 19
2. Tequila Sunrise, page 14
3. Chi Chi, page 14
4. Cranapple Perk, page 36
5. Harvey Wallbanger, page 17
6. Strawberry Margarita, page 18
7. Iced Tea, page 74
8. Mixed Citrus Punch, page 46
9. Forest Fantasy, page 16
10. Dessert Tea, page 72
11. Blueberry Shake, page 61
12. Pineapple Ade, page 40

Background Tile Courtesy Of: Panache Ceramic Industries
Glassware Courtesy Of: Le Gnome And The Bay
Flower Vase Courtesy Of: The Bay

Back Cover   Front Cover

Printed In Canada

The Jean Paré Story

Jean Paré grew up understanding that the combination of family, friends and home cooking is the essence of a good life. From her mother she learned to appreciate good cooking, while her father praised even her earliest attempts. When she left home she took with her many acquired family recipes, her love of cooking and her intriguing desire to read recipe books like novels!

In 1963, when her four children had all reached school age, Jean volunteered to cater to the 50th anniversary of the Vermilion School of Agriculture, now Lakeland College. Working out of her home, Jean prepared a dinner for over 1000 people which launched a flourishing catering operation that continued for over eighteen years. During that time she was provided with countless opportunities to test new ideas with immediate feedback—resulting in empty plates and contented customers! Whether preparing cocktail sandwiches for a house party or serving a hot meal for 1500 people, Jean Paré earned a reputation for good food, courteous service and reasonable prices.

"Why don't you write a cookbook?" Time and again, as requests for her recipes mounted, Jean was asked that question. Jean's response was to team up with her son, Grant Lovig, in the fall of 1980 to form Company's Coming Publishing Limited. April 14, 1981, marked the debut of "150 DELICIOUS SQUARES", the first Company's Coming cookbook in what soon would become Canada's most popular cookbook series. By 1995, sales had surpassed ten million cookbooks.

Jean Paré's operation has grown from the early days of working out of a spare bedroom in her home to operating a large and fully equipped test kitchen in Vermilion, Alberta, near the home she and her husband Larry built. Full-time staff has grown steadily to include marketing personnel located in major cities across Canada plus selected U.S. markets. Home Office is located in Edmonton, Alberta, where distribution, accounting and administration functions are headquartered in the company's own 20,000 square foot facility. Growth continues with the recent addition of the Recipe Factory, a 2700 square foot test kitchen and photography studio located in Edmonton.

Company's Coming cookbooks are now distributed throughout Canada and the United States plus numerous overseas markets, all under the guidance of Jean's daughter, Gail Lovig. The series is published in English and French, plus a Spanish language edition is available in Mexico. Familiar and trusted Company's Coming-style recipes are now available in a variety of formats in addition to the bestselling soft cover series.

Jean Paré's approach to cooking has always called for quick and easy recipes using everyday ingredients. She continues to gain new supporters by adhering to what she calls "the golden rule of cooking": never share a recipe you wouldn't use yourself. It's an approach that works—*ten million times over!*

Table Of Contents

Foreword

Hospitality begins with food and drink. Beverages are perfect for parties and are especially welcome when served to guests as they arrive at any social gathering. Beverages are an essential part of informal get-togethers with family and friends.

Entertain with either alcohol or alcohol-free drinks. It is a good idea to offer your guests a choice. Learn colorfully delicious ways of making festive drinks without alcohol. If you prefer alcohol in a punch, measure the total volume of the punch then add 1/4 of that amount of alcohol (such as vodka, gin or white rum).

Cocktails and mock cocktails are not only refreshing but also attractive, showing off your fancy glasses and delicate stemware. With lots of ice and imaginative garnishes it will be easy to make an impression on everyone. The addition of an elegant ice ring to a punch will make it a focal point on your buffet table.

BEVERAGES contains an assortment of blender drinks, coffee combinations and punches. Some are hot, some are cold, but all are delicious. Try Café Latté or Frosty Café Au Lait with your best friend. For a smooth after-dinner drink, serve Coffee Malt or Brandy Mint Cream. Steaming Cranapple Perk will warm up those cold winter nights. An ice cold pitcher of Lemonade or Pineapple Ade will cool off those hot summer days.

BEVERAGES offers a wide variety of flavors to quench any thirst. For small gatherings or large crowds, you can rely upon the beverage recipes in this book to add sparkle to your day. Cheers!

Jean Paré

Glossary Of Glasses

The glasses in which you serve your drinks are every bit as important as the ingredients, the taste and the garnishes. With such a variety it is essential to know which drink should be served in which glass. In some cases there are reasons for the choice of glass. A Martini glass is held by its stem so the hand does not warm the glass. A brandy snifter is rested in the palm to warm the drink and release its aroma. The narrowness of a champagne flute is a design to preserve the bubbles. Pictured on the next two pages is a selection of glasses to help in choosing the most suitable glass.

1. **Collins Glass:** A tall, straight-sided glass. Holds 1¼ to 2 cups (300 to 500 mL). Excellent for drinks like Tom Collins.

2. **Large Goblet:** Varies greatly in shape and size. Used for serving water or wine spritzers or any exotic drink. Holds 1 to 2 cups (250 to 500 mL).

3. **Brandy Balloon Snifter:** For straight brandy or brandy-based drinks. Holds ¾ to 3 cups (175 to 750 mL).

4. **Red Wine Glass:** Slightly larger than the white wine glass. Holds 1 to 1¼ cups (250 to 300 mL).

5. **Martini (Cocktail) Glass:** A stemmed, triangular-shaped, wide-rimmed glass used for martinis or other cocktails. Holds ½ to ¾ cup (125 to 175 mL).

6. **Champagne Flute:** A tall, stemmed glass used for champagne and sparkling wine drinks. Holds ¾ to 1 cup (175 to 250 mL).

(continued on next page)

Glossary Of Glasses (cont'd.)

7. Highball Glass: A smaller glass than the Collins. General type of glass and can be used for many types of drinks. Holds 1 to 1¼ cups (250 to 300 mL).

8. Double Cocktail Glass or Champagne Saucer: A large, rounded cocktail glass used for serving cream-based or slushy drinks such as a Daiquiri. Holds ¾ to 1¼ cups (175 to 300 mL).

9. **Liqueur Glass.** Used for serving short, straight drinks. Holds 2 to 4 tbsp. (30 to 60 mL).

10. **White Wine Glass.** A bit smaller than the red wine glass. Holds ¾ to 1 cup (175 to 250 mL).

11. **Old Fashioned Glass:** A short, straight-sided tumbler. Holds ½ to 1 cup (125 to 250 mL).

Garnishes

Cinnamon Stick Stack

Choose 3 to 5 cinnamon sticks similar in length. Wash and dry smooth-skinned orange. Using citrus stripper, cut a long, continuous coil of peel from about ½ the orange. Wrap the peel around cinnamon sticks. Tie into knot. Perfect to garnish a punch.

Melon Skewers

Choose any combination of honeydew, cantaloupe or watermelon. Remove seeds. Using melon baller, cut out flesh by pushing the baller into melon and twisting in circle. Make as many balls as needed. Thread three balls onto each cocktail pick, alternating colors.

**1. Melon Skewers   2. Banana Swords
3. Cucumber Wheels**

Cucumber Wheels

Wash and dry whole, unpeeled English cucumber. Using citrus stripper, remove strips of skin lengthwise down cucumber, spacing strips evenly apart (¼ to ½ inch, 6 to 12 mm). Cut cucumber into thin slices. Make slit in cucumber to sit on rim of glass.

LEMON WHEELS: Use lemon instead of cucumber.
LIME WHEELS: Use lime instead of cucumber.
ORANGE WHEELS: Use orange instead of cucumber.

Citrus Knots

Choose firm, smooth-skinned lemon, lime or orange. Wash and dry. Using citrus stripper, remove long, continuous coil of peel from fruit. Tie peel into knot and drop into drink.

Banana Swords

Choose firm banana. Peel and cut into ½ inch (12 mm) slices. Cover slices with lemon juice to prevent browning. Thread 3 to 4 slices onto cocktail pick, spacing them evenly. Dust with grated nutmeg or chocolate.

Strawberry Fan

Choose firm, nicely-shaped strawberries with leaves. Wash and dry. Using sharp paring knife, slice strawberries vertically from bottom to top being careful not to cut right through top of strawberry. Make about 5 parallel cuts.Gently spread slices apart to make fan. Hang strawberry over rim of glass.

Lemon Peel Spiral

Choose firm, smooth-skinned lemon. Wash and dry. Using citrus stripper, remove long continuous coil of lemon peel from entire length of lemon. Place a few ice cubes in glass. Wind spiral around inside of glass. Add more ice cubes after each curl to secure the peel. Pour clear or light colored beverage over.

Blueberry & Lemon Twist

Cut thin lemon slice in half. Push blueberry onto cocktail pick. Place lemon slice half on cocktail pick through skin near cut edge. Put another blueberry on pick. Curl the lemon half around blueberry like a sail. Repeat with second half, forming an "S" shape around the blueberries. Top with 4th blueberry.

Green & Red Apple Chevrons

Use green and red apple similar in size and shape. Wash and dry. Using sharp paring knife, cut small wedge from side of each apple. Using a gentle sawing motion, continue cutting progressively larger wedges (each $1/8$ inch, 3 mm) larger than the last. Remove each wedge as it is cut and dip in lemon juice to prevent browning. Alternate green and red wedge for each glass. Make slit in flesh of bottom wedge to hook over rim of glass.

1. Blueberry & Lemon Twist
2. Strawberry Fan   **3. Apple Chevrons**

Brown Cow
Great taste of Kahlua. A satisfyingly cool drink.

		Crushed ice	Fill tall or old fashioned glass
45 mL	1½ oz.	Kahlua	with crushed ice. Add
		Milk	Kahlua. Pour in milk to fill.
			Serves 1.

Pictured on page 13.

Shirley Temple
A variation of an old favorite.

		Crushed ice or ice cubes	Fill tall glass with ice. Pour
10 mL	2 tsp.	Grenadine	grenadine, lemon juice,
10 mL	2 tsp.	Lemon juice, fresh or bottled	Sugar Syrup and ginger ale
15 mL	1 tbsp.	Sugar Syrup, below	over ice. Stir lightly with
		Ginger ale, to fill	swizzle stick. More grenadine
			may be added for a deeper
			color. Makes 1 drink.

Pictured on page 13.

Sugar Syrup
This sweetener is already dissolved. Use to sweeten tea and coffee drinks and others as well.

		Water	Heat and stir water and
250 mL	1 cup	Water	sugar in saucepan until
500 mL	2 cups	Granulated sugar	boiling. Boil slowly for 5
			minutes. Cool. Keeps almost
			indefinitely. Makes a scant 2
			cups (500 mL).

Garnish Tip

Cherry Mint Slice

Choose orange and lemon.
(Orange should be larger than
lemon). Cut thin slice from both.
Make slit in the center of each.
Place on rim of glass. Take
maraschino cherry with stem
and place two small mint leaves
in the hole where the cherry has
been pitted. Make a tiny slit in
opposite side of cherry. Place
beside lemon.

Glassware Courtesy Of:
Le Gnome

Shirley Temple, page 12

Brown Cow, page 12

Tequila Sunrise

If you watch closely, you will see the sunrise in this cocktail.

4	4	Ice cubes	Drop cubes into tall narrow glass. Add tequila and orange juice. Stir.
45-60 mL	1½-2oz.	Tequila	
		Prepared orange juice, to fill	
1	1	Maraschino cherry	Secure cherry and orange slice on rim of glass before adding grenadine.
1	1	Orange slice	
15-25 mL	1-1½ tbsp.	Grenadine	Drop grenadine all at once into center of glass so it will fall to the bottom. It will rise reminiscent of a sunrise. Makes 1 drink.

Pictured on back cover.

Chi Chi

A creamy concoction to sip by the pool or on the deck.

45 mL	1½ oz.	Vodka	Combine first 4 ingredients in blender. Process until smooth.
30 mL	2 tbsp.	Thick coconut milk or coconut cream	
125 mL	½ cup	Pineapple juice	
250 mL	1 cup	Crushed Ice	
		Pineapple chunk (fresh or canned) or maraschino cherry, for garnish	Garnish with pineapple or cherry. Serves 1.

VIRGIN CHI CHI: Omit vodka. Add an extra 3 tbsp. (50 mL) pineapple juice.

Pictured on back cover.

Mai Tai

It is necessary to use all of these ingredients if you want to be a true Hawaiian wahini (wah-HEE-nee) or kane (KAH-nay).

		Crushed ice	Fill old fashioned glass with ice. Add light rum, Curaçao, lemon juice, pineapple juice and orange juice. Stir.
25 mL	¾ oz.	Light rum	
7 mL	¼ oz.	Curaçao or Triple Sec	
50 mL	3 tbsp.	Lemon juice	
50 mL	3 tbsp.	Pineapple juice	
50 mL	3 tbsp.	Prepared orange juice	
25 mL	¾ oz.	Dark rum	Float dark rum on top.
		Small orchid, cherry or pineapple	Garnish. Makes 1 drink.

Pictured on page 17.

Piña Colada

A wonderful afternoon cocktail is creamy PEEN-yuh koh-LAH-duh. For fun, try serving in a coconut shell.

45 mL	1½ oz.	Light rum	Combine all ingredients in blender. Process well. Pour into large goblet. Garnish as desired. Makes 1 drink.
50 mL	3 tbsp.	Thick coconut milk or coconut cream	
125 mL	½ cup	Pineapple juice (or other tropical juice)	
25 mL	1½ tbsp.	Sugar Syrup, page 12	
250 mL	1 cup	Crushed ice or small ice cubes	

Pictured on page 17.

VIRGIN PIÑA COLADA: Omit rum. Add an extra 3 tbsp. (50 mL) pineapple juice.

Tom Collins *Always elegant!*

25 mL	1½ tbsp.	Lemon juice, fresh or bottled	Shake lemon juice, sugar and gin in shaker.
10 mL	2 tsp.	Berry or fine granulated sugar	
45 mL	1½ oz.	Gin	
		Crushed ice	Fill tall glass with crushed ice.
		Club soda, to fill	Pour shaker contents over ice. Fill glass with club soda.
		Maraschino cherry	Garnish with cherry and
		Thin lemon slice	lemon. Makes 1 cocktail.

Pictured on page 17.

Forest Fantasy *Sparkling clear green drink. Mild creamy mint flavor.*

3-4	3-4	Ice cubes	Drop ice cubes into old
45 mL	1½ oz.	Crème de Menthe (green)	fashioned glass. Add Crème
30 mL	1 oz.	Crème de Cacao (white)	de Menthe, Crème de
5 mL	1 tsp.	Lime juice, fresh or bottled	Cacao, lime juice and Sugar
10 mL	2 tsp.	Sugar Syrup, page 12	Syrup. Stir.
125 mL	½ cup	Club soda	Add club soda. Stir gently.
			Garnish as desired. Makes 1 drink.

Pictured on front cover.

Harvey Wallbanger

An old timer. Orange juice mixture topped with Galliano.

3-4	3-4	Ice cubes
45 mL	1½ oz.	Vodka
175 mL	¾ cup	Orange juice
10 mL	2 tsp.	Galliano

Pictured on front cover.

Drop ice cubes into old fashioned glass. Add vodka and orange juice. Float Galliano on top. Makes 1 drink.

Mai Tai, page 15   **Tom Collins, page 16**   **Piña Colada, page 15**

Glassware Courtesy Of: Stokes And Eaton's

Margarita

A summer holiday drink. Try the variations as well.

		Salted Rim, page 29	Salt rim of glass using lime wedge.
45 mL	1½ oz.	Tequila	Combine next 5 ingredients in cocktail shaker. Shake well.
15 mL	½ oz.	Triple Sec or Cointreau	
30 mL	1 oz.	Lime juice	
10-15 mL	2-3 tsp.	Sugar Syrup, page 12	
125 mL	½ cup	Crushed ice	

Crushed ice or ice cubes to fill glass (bowl type is best)

Strain over crushed ice in glass. Serve with a straw. Makes 1 drink.

STRAWBERRY MARGARITA: Add 10 frozen strawberries, cut up, to blender with tequila, 1½ tbsp. (25 mL) Sugar Syrup and crushed ice. Omit lime juice. Process until smooth. Pour over crushed ice in glass. Serve with straw. Slushy, thick and smooth.

FROZEN MARGARITA: Process tequila, Triple Sec, lime juice, Sugar Syrup and 1½ cups (375 mL) crushed ice in blender until slushy. Serve with straw.

Pictured on front cover.

Caesar

This is one of the most variable drinks. Some like it hot with spice while others prefer it quite mild. Use more or less spice to taste.

		Salted Rim, page 29.	Salt rim of glass using lemon wedge and celery salt,
3-4	3-4	Ice cubes	Add next 8 ingredients in order given. Stir.
45 mL	1 1/2 oz.	Vodka	
4-6	4-6	Drops of hot pepper sauce (such as Tabasco)	
0.5 mL	1/8 tsp.	Worcestershire sauce	
		Celery salt, light sprinkle	
		Salt, light sprinkle	
		Pepper, light sprinkle	
		Clamato juice, to fill	
		Celery stick (long enough to stand above rim) or lime slice, for garnish.	Add celery stick or lime slice. Serves 1.

Pictured on back cover.

VIRGIN CAESAR: Omit vodka.

BLOODY MARY: Use tomato juice instead of clamato juice. Celery stick is optional.

VIRGIN BLOODY MARY: Omit vodka.

Daiquiri

Great on a hot day.

		Salted Rim, page 29	Salt rim of glass using lime wedge.
60 mL	2 oz.	White rum	Combine next 4 ingredients in cocktail shaker. Shake well. Strain into bowl type glass.
30 mL	2 tbsp.	Lime juice, fresh or bottled	
10-15 mL	2-3 tsp.	Sugar Syrup, page 12	
125 mL	½ cup	Crushed ice	

DAIQUIRI ON ICE: Strain into bowl type glass filled with crushed ice.

STRAWBERRY DAIQUIRI: Combine rum, lime juice, Sugar Syrup, crushed ice and 10 frozen strawberries, cut up, in blender. Process until smooth. Pour into bowl type glass filled with crushed ice. Delicious.

Stemware Courtesy Of: Stokes

Pictured on this page.

Frappé   *Fra-PAY is a refreshing cold coffee drink.*

250 mL	1 cup	Water	Process first 4 ingredients in
175 mL	¾ cup	Milk	blender for about 10
15 mL	1 tbsp.	Instant coffee granules	seconds.
5 mL	1 tsp.	Granulated sugar (or to taste)	
6-8	6-8	Ice cubes	Divide ice cubes between 2 glasses. Pour blender
		Pictured on page 23.	contents over ice. Makes 2 drinks.

Frosty Café Au Lait   *Frothy tan-colored drink with a sprinkle of chocolate or cinnamon. Makes as much foam as liquid.*

250 mL	1 cup	Cold strong coffee	Process first 4 ingredients in
15 mL	1 tbsp.	Granulated sugar	blender until blended.
15 mL	1 tbsp.	Cocoa	
250 mL	1 cup	Skim evaporated milk	
250 mL	1 cup	Crushed ice	Add crushed ice. Process to blend. Pour into 3 tall glasses.
		Ground cinnamon or grated chocolate, sprinkle	Sprinkle with cinnamon or chocolate. Makes 3 drinks, each about 5 oz. (150 mL) of drink and as much foam.

Coffee Nog *Nice and creamy looking.*

2 L	8 cups	Cold coffee	Pour coffee and rum into
500 mL	2 cups	Amber or light rum	punch bowl. Stir.
1 L	4 cups	Vanilla ice cream	Add ice cream in spoonfuls or chunks. Stir. Makes 14 cups (3.5 L).

Iced Café Latté *Great way to use leftover coffee.*

Ice cubes or crushed ice Milk Cold espresso coffee	Fill tall glass with ice. Add milk to make ⅔ full, then fill with coffee.
Sugar Syrup, page 12, to taste	Sweeten with Sugar Syrup, page 12, if desired.

ICED CAPPUCCINO: Use ½ milk and ½ cold espresso coffee. Sweeten if desired.

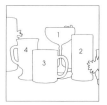

1. **Brandy Mint Cream, page 25**
2. **G'Morning Sunshine, page 25**
3. **Frappé, page 21**
4. **Coffee Frosty, page 24**

Glassware And Vases Courtesy Of:
Stokes And Zeller's

Coffee Malt

You will need lots of this. Serve as an after-dinner drink instead of a liqueur or as a dessert drink. Kids love it.

60 mL	¹/₄ cup	Milk	Process all 4 ingredients in
250 mL	1 cup	Coffee ice cream, cut up	blender for 15 to 20 seconds.
30 mL	2 tbsp.	Malted milk powder (such	Pour into two 6 oz. (200 mL)
		as Ovaltine)	glasses. Makes 1¹/₄ cups
1 mL	¹/₄ tsp.	Vanilla	(300 mL). Serves 2.

Island Frost

Now this is refreshing. Add more ice cream for a thicker shake if desired.

250 mL	1 cup	Cold strong coffee	Combine coffee, juice and
125 mL	¹/₂ cup	Pineapple juice	ice cream in blender.
250 mL	1 cup	Coffee ice cream	Process until smooth.
4	4	Coffee Ice Cubes,	Pour over coffee ice cubes
		page 51	in glasses. Makes 2¹/₂ cups
			(625 mL).

Coffee Frosty

Refreshing to be sure. If using chocolate ice cream, the coffee flavor is more subtle.

250 mL	1 cup	Cold strong coffee	Process coffee and ice
250 mL	1 cup	Espresso flake ice cream	cream in blender until
		(or chocolate)	blended.
4	4	Coffee Ice Cubes,	Place 2 ice cubes in each of
		page 51	two 12 oz. (375 mL) glasses.
			Pour ice cream mixture over
			ice. Makes 2 servings.

Pictured on page 23.

Brandy Mint Cream

Frothy, thick and smooth. Stays thick for at least one hour. A good after dinner drink. Use white or green liqueur for different shades.

1 L	1 qt.	Vanilla ice cream, softened	Spoon ice cream into bowl. Add brandy and Crème de Menthe. Beat on medium-low to mix. Pour into fancy glasses such as parfait, champagne or wine. Makes about 7 cups (1.75 L).
125 mL	½ cup	Brandy	
60 mL	¼ cup	Crème de Menthe, green or white	

Pictured on page 23.

G'Morning Sunshine

Creamy orange flavor. A bit reminiscent of a creamsicle.

1 L	4 cups	Chilled milk	Stir milk, juice and sugar together in pitcher. Mixture will be a bit frothy by time sugar is dissolved.
60 mL	¼ cup	Frozen concentrated orange juice, thawed	
60 mL	¼ cup	Granulated sugar	
		Ground nutmeg, sprinkle (optional)	Pour into glasses. Sprinkle with nutmeg if desired. Makes 4 cups (1 L).

Pictured on page 23.

Orange Mocha Coffee *Enough flavors here to suit everyone.*

Orange Mocha Mix

125 mL	½ cup	Instant coffee granules	Measure all 6 ingredients
75 mL	⅓ cup	Granulated sugar	into blender. Process until
30 mL	2 tbsp.	Cocoa	powdered. Makes 1⅛ cups
125 mL	½ cup	Skim milk powder	(280 mL).
60 mL	¼ cup	Powdered coffee whitener	
50 mL	3 tbsp.	Sweetened orange crystals (such as Tang)	

To Serve

30 mL	2 tbsp.	Orange Mocha Mix, above	Place mix in mug. Fill mug with boiling water. Stir.
250 mL	1 cup	Boiling water	Makes 1 serving.

Café Latté

*It will be difficult to choose which to have,
the Ka-fay LAH-tay or the Café Au Lait.
Good anytime drinks.*

500 mL	**2 cups**	Hot espresso coffee
500 mL	**2 cups**	Milk
		Granulated sugar, to taste (optional)

While preparing coffee, pour milk into small saucepan. Heat until hot but not scalding. It is best to have a thermometer. Temperature of hot milk should read 140° to 160°F (60° to 71°C) to be at its frothy best. Beat with whisk until foamy. Pour ½ cup (125 mL) each coffee and milk simultaneously into each of 4 latté glasses or mugs. Top with the foam. Add sugar if desired.

Sweetened cocoa powder or ground cinnamon

Sprinkle with sweetened cocoa powder or cinnamon. Makes 4 servings of 1 cup (250 mL) each.

Pictured on page 29.

CAFÉ AU LAIT: Ka-fay Oh LAY is made the same as above except use regular coffee and scalded milk.

Variation: These are extra good using light cream rather than milk.

Spanish Coffee

A special coffee served in a sugar frosted glass.

		Sugared Rim, page 29	Sugar rim of glass and set aside.
30 mL	1 oz.	Kahlua or Crème de Cacao	Pour Kahlua and brandy into glass. Fill with hot coffee to ½ inch (12 mm) from rim.
15 mL	½ oz.	Brandy Hot coffee	
		Whipped cream or frozen whipped topping, thawed	Top with whipped cream to the brim. Do not stir. Sip coffee through cream. Makes 1 drink.

Pictured on page 29.

Canadian Coffee

Maple flavored from a maple leaf country.

250 mL	1 cup	Hot coffee	Pour coffee into large measuring cup with pouring spout.
30 mL	1 oz.	Maple liqueur	Add liqueur and whiskey. Stir. Pour into 2 glass mugs.
30 mL	1 oz.	Rye whiskey (such as Canadian Club)	
		Whipped cream (spray type works well)	Top with whipped cream. Makes two 5 oz. (75 mL) servings.

1

2

Chocolate Frost

Grate semisweet chocolate baking square over top of drink or grate into container. Use spoon to sprinkle. If you use your fingers, the chocolate will melt. Grate fine or larger if desired. A great finishing touch over whipped topping.

Salted Or Sugared Rim

Put salt or sugar into bowl or saucer to a depth of ⅛ inch (3 mm). Put lemon or lime juice into another bowl or saucer. Dip rim of glass into lemon or lime juice or rub rim with lemon or lime wedge. Dip rim of glass into sugar, salt or celery salt, covering rim evenly. If coating is uneven, dip into salt or sugar again.

Note: Regular, medium or coarse salt may be used. Regular, fine or super fine sugar may be used.

1. **Spanish Coffee, page 28**
2. **Café Latté, page 27**

Glassware Courtesy Of: The Bay

Tip

To make milk layers in Café Latté, pour milk and foam into mug. Slowly pour in hot coffee using a spoon to guide coffee into mug.

Chococcino

With this dry mix on hand, it takes no time to have a cuppa.

Chococcino Mix

250 mL	1 cup	Instant coffee granules
250 mL	1 cup	Granulated sugar
250 mL	1 cup	Powdered coffee whitener
125 mL	½ cup	Cocoa
2 mL	½ tsp.	Ground cinnamon
2 mL	½ tsp.	Ground nutmeg

Combine all ingredients in blender. Process until powdered. Makes 2⅔ cups (650 mL).

To Serve

30 mL	2 tbsp.	Chococcino Mix, above
250 mL	1 cup	Boiling water

Measure mix into mug. Add boiling water. Stir. Makes 1 serving.

AMARETTO CHOCOCCINO: Omit cinnamon and nutmeg. Use Amaretto powdered coffee whitener instead of plain.

IRISH CREAM CHOCOCCINO: Omit cinnamon and nutmeg. Use Irish Cream powdered coffee whitener instead of plain.

MINT CHOCOCCINO: Omit cinnamon and nutmeg. Use Mint powdered coffee whitener instead of plain.

HAZELNUT CHOCOCCINO: Omit cinnamon and nutmeg. Use Hazelnut powdered coffee whitener instead of plain.

Mocha Coffee

A good drink, dark brown in color. Coffee and chocolate.

15 mL	1 tbsp.	Instant coffee granules	Measure first 5 ingredients in large measuring cup with pouring spout. Stir.
15 mL	1 tbsp.	Granulated sugar	
60 mL	¼ cup	Skim milk powder	
10 mL	2 tsp.	Powdered coffee whitener	
15 mL	1 tbsp.	Cocoa	
500 mL	2 cups	Boiling water	Add boiling water. Stir well. Pour into 2 mugs.
50 mL	3 tbsp.	Whipped cream or topping	Top with whipped cream. Sprinkle with cinnamon or chocolate.
		Ground cinnamon or chocolate, light sprinkle	

Pictured on this page.

Variation: For a sweeter drink, omit cocoa and add same amount of instant sweetened chocolate powder.

SPICED MOCHA COFFEE: Stir in a wee pinch of ground cinnamon.

Glass Mug Courtesy Of: Stokes
Glass Saucer Courtesy Of: Le Gnome

Café Brûlot

This Ka-fay Broo-LOH has a taste of brandy with a light citrus flavor. A flambé coffee.

1	1	Small orange	Using a vegetable peeler, peel orange and lemon in strips. Slice in long narrow pieces. Save both orange and lemon to use another time. Place peel, cloves, cinnamon and sugar cubes in brûlot bowl or chafing dish.
1	1	Small lemon	
10	10	Whole cloves	
3	3	Cinnamon sticks (4 inches, 10 cm, each in length)	
12-16	12-16	Sugar cubes	
250 mL	1 cup	Brandy	Add brandy. Heat until brandy is warm. Ignite with match. Do not heat brandy too hot or it won't ignite. Stir flaming brandy until sugar dissolves.
1 L	4 cups	Hot strong coffee	Gradually add hot coffee. Keep stirring gently until flame goes out. Laddle or strain into cups. Makes 5 cups (1.25 L).

Pictured on page 33.

Cappuccino Coffee
A favorite coffee with a hint of orange.

Cappuccino Mix

125 mL	½ cup	Instant coffee granules	Combine all 5 ingredients in
175 mL	¾ cup	Granulated sugar	blender. Process until
175 mL	¾ cup	Powdered coffee	powdered. Makes 2 cups
		whitener	(500 mL).
25 mL	5 tsp.	Orange-flavored drink	
		crystals (such as Tang)	
75 mL	⅓ cup	Powdered skim milk	

To Serve

30 mL	2 tbsp.	Cappuccino Mix, above	Measure mix into mug. Add
250 mL	1 cup	Boiling water	boiling water. Stir. Makes 1
			serving.

Café Brûlot, page 32   Bodem Coffee Pot Courtesy Of: Enchanted Kitchen   Glass Mug Courtesy Of: The Bay

Irish Coffee

Adjust whiskey according to taste.

		Sugared Rim, page 29	Sugar glass rims.
45 mL	**1½ oz.**	Irish whiskey	Combine Irish whiskey and
5 mL	**1 tsp.**	Granulated sugar	sugar in Irish coffee glass.
175 mL	**¾ cup**	Hot strong coffee	Add coffee. Stir.
15-30 mL	**1-2 tbsp.**	Whipped cream or topping	Pour whipped cream on spoon held over coffee, allowing it to run off to fill to rim of glass. Do not stir. Drink coffee through cream. Makes 1 serving.

Special Ending

But why does it have to end?

		Sugared Rim, page 29	Sugar glass rim and set aside.
15 mL	**½ oz.**	Brandy	Measure brandy, Kahlua
15 mL	**½ oz.**	Kahlua	and Crème de Cacao into
15 mL	**½ oz.**	Crème de Cacao (dark)	glass. This may be done ahead and completed at the last minute.
		Hot coffee	Fill glass with coffee. Top
		Whipped cream or topping	with whipped cream. Do not stir. Sip coffee through cream. Makes 1 drink.

Grape Tea

Similar in good taste no matter which color of grape juice you use.

2 L	8 cups	Water	Combine first amount of water and cloves in large saucepan. Bring to a boil. Cover. Boil gently for 1 minute. Let steep for 10 minutes.
24	24	Whole cloves	
125 mL	½ cup	Lemon juice, fresh or bottled	Add lemon juice, sugar and grape juice Stir. Keep hot over low heat.
375 mL	1½ cups	Granulated sugar (or more to taste)	
500 mL	2 cups	Grape juice, white or purple	
1.5 L	6 cups	Boiling water	Pour boiling water over tea bags in separate saucepan. Cover. Steep for 10 minutes. Add to grape juice mixture pressing tea bags to get out liquid. Remove cloves with slotted spoon. Serve tea hot. Makes 16 cups (4 L).
4	4	Orange pekoe tea bags	

Skiers' Wine

Welcome your sports enthusiasts with mulled wine.

500 mL	2 cups	Prepared orange juice	Combine first 5 ingredients
75 mL	⅓ cup	Lemon juice, fresh or	in heavy saucepan. Heat
		bottled	slowly, stirring often. Keep
125 mL	½ cup	Granulated sugar	hot for about 15 minutes
2	2	Cinnamon sticks,	until spices release flavors.
		(4 inches,10 cm, each	May be strained if desired
		in length), broken up	and returned to saucepan.
6	6	Whole cloves	
1 L	4 cups	Red wine (or alcohol-free	Add wine. Heat through but
		wine)	don't boil. Serve hot. Makes
			6½ cups (1.5 L).

Pictured on page 37.

Cranapple Perk

. . . and you thought that only coffee gets percolated.

3 L	12 cups	Apple juice or cider	Combine apple juice,
2 L	8 cups	Cranberry cocktail	cranberry cocktail, wine and
1 L	4 cups	Rosé or Burgundy wine (or	lemon juice in bottom of
		alcohol-free red wine)	percolator. Position stem
30 mL	2 tbsp.	Lemon juice, fresh or	and basket.
		bottled	
175 mL	¾ cup	Brown sugar, packed	Add remaining 4 ingredients
		Salt, sprinkle	to basket. Cover. Run
20	20	Whole cloves	through cycle. Makes 24
5	5	Cinnamon sticks,	cups (6 L).
		(4 inches,10 cm, each	
		in length), broken up	**Pictured on back cover.**

Hot Chocolate Mix

Makes a creamy and flavorful hot chocolate.

Dry Mix

250 mL	1 cup	Instant hot chocolate mix (such as Quik)	
750 mL	3 cups	Powdered skim milk	
100 mL	6 tbsp.	Powdered coffee whitener	
60 mL	1/4 cup	Icing (confectioner's) sugar	

Measure all 4 ingredients into bowl. Stir well. This may be run through blender if desired to make more powdery. Makes 4 cups (1 L) dry mix.

To Serve

75 mL	1/3 cup	Dry Mix, above
250 mL	1 cup	Boiling water

Measure 1/3 cup (75 mL) Dry Mix into 8 oz. (250 mL) mug. Add boiling water to fill. Stir. Makes 1 serving.

Skiers' Wine, page 36

MINT HOT CHOCOLATE: To 1 mug of hot chocolate, add 1 to 1 1/2 oz. (30 to 45 mL) peppermint schnapps. Top with whipped cream or pressurized topping. Sprinkle with grated or powdered chocolate.

Mug Courtesy Of: The Bay

Orange Fluff

Very fluffy and frothy. Mild creamy orange flavor. Tiny bubbles everywhere.

250 mL	1 cup	Prepared orange juice	Pour orange juice into blender. Add dry topping mix and sugar. Process on high for 2 minutes.
1	1	Envelope topping mix, (such as Dream Whip) added dry	
30 mL	2 tbsp.	Icing (confectioner's) sugar (optional)	
250 mL	1 cup	Club soda	Add club soda. Stir gently. Makes 2½ cups (625 mL).

Pictured on page 39.

Mint Cooler

A real refresher. Mild mint flavor. Light clear color. Surprisingly good.

500 mL	2 cups	Mint leaves, bruised (see Note)	Combine all 3 ingredients in bowl. Cover. Let steep for 3 hours. Remove mint leaves. Taste for sugar, stirring in up to ¼ cup (60 mL) more if desired for sweetness. Chill mixture. Serve over ice in glasses. Makes 8 cups (2 L).
2 L	8 cups	Boiling water	
300 mL	1¼ cups	Granulated sugar	

1. Orange Fluff, page 38
2. Lemonade, page 40
3. Sangria, page 41
4. Grape Lemonade, page 41

Glassware Courtesy Of:
Le Gnome, The Glasshouse And The Royal Doulton Store

Note: To bruise, place mint leaves in plastic bag. Smash with bottom of glass.

Lemonade
The drink you think of on a hot day.

Lemon Concentrate

2.5 L	10 cups	Granulated sugar	Measure sugar and water
1.5 L	6 cups	Water	into saucepan. Heat and stir until boiling. Boil for 5 minutes. Remove from heat.
750 mL	3 cups	Fresh lemon juice (about 12 lemons)	Stir in lemon juice and citric acid. Cool. Store in container
30 mL	2 tbsp.	Citric acid (drug store)	in refrigerator. Makes 11½ cups (2.88 L) concentrate.

To Serve

2-3	2-3	Ice cubes	Drop ice cubes into large
60 mL	¼ cup	Lemon Concentrate, above	glass. Add Lemon Concentrate and water.
250 mL	1 cup	Cold water	Stir. Makes 1 serving.

Pictured on page 39.

Pineapple Ade
With a bit of orange flavor too. Deep yellow color.

375 mL	1½ cups	Water	Stir water and sugar together
75 mL	⅓ cup	Granulated sugar	in pitcher until sugar is dissolved.
750 mL	3 cups	Pineapple juice	Add all 3 juices. Chill. Pour
		Juice of 2 oranges	over ice. Makes about 7
		Juice of 2 lemons	cups (1.75 L).

Pictured on front cover.

Sangria
Triple recipe to fill a punch bowl.

125 mL	½ cup	Brandy	Pour brandy into large bowl.
75 mL	⅓ cup	Granulated sugar	Add sugar. Stir to dissolve
1	1	Medium orange, sliced	sugar. Add orange, lemon
1	1	Lemon, sliced	and lime slices. Let stand for
1	1	Lime, sliced	1½ hours.
750 mL	3 cups	Red wine, chilled	Add wine. Strain into large pitcher. Reserve fruit slices.
500 mL	2 cups	Club soda, chilled	When ready to serve add club soda. Stir gently.
		Ice cubes	Drop 2 to 4 ice cubes into
		Reserved fruit slices	glasses. Add a slice or two reserved fruit slices to each glass. Add 2 or 3 slices to pitcher also. Fill glasses with Sangria. Makes 7 cups (1.75 L).

Pictured on page 39.

Grape Lemonade
Good taste whether using light or dark grape juice.

750 mL	3 cups	Water	Pour water and sugar into
75 mL	⅓ cup	Granulated sugar	pitcher. Stir to dissolve sugar.
500 mL	2 cups	Grape juice, white or purple	Add grape juice and lemon juice. Stir. Taste for sweetness
125 mL	½ cup	Lemon juice, fresh or bottled	adding a bit more sugar if desired. A bit more water may be added but add slowly so as not to make too weak. Makes about 6 cups (1.35 L).

Pictured on page 39.

Cranberry Punch

Refreshing rose colored drink.
Easy to double recipe.

1.25 L	5 cups	Cranberry cocktail	Stir cranberry cocktail and
¹/₂ × 341 mL	¹/₂ × 12 oz.	Frozen concentrated	concentrated orange juice
		orange juice, thawed	together in punch bowl.
1.25 L	5 cups	Ginger ale	Add ginger ale just before
			serving. Stir gently.

Pictured on page 43.

Garnish as desired. Makes 10¹/₂ cups (2.6 L).

Season's Brew

A delectable hot drink, full of spicy taste and aroma. Use a percolator or a saucepan. Increase recipe as needed.

1 L	4 cups	Cranberry cocktail	Pour cranberry cocktail and
1 L	4 cups	Pineapple juice	pineapple juice into bottom of percolator. Insert stem and basket.
75 mL	¹/₃ cup	Granulated sugar	Put remaining ingredients into
1 mL	¹/₄ tsp.	Salt	basket. Run through cycle. If
10 mL	2 tsp.	Whole allspice	using saucepan, put
15 mL	1 tbsp.	Whole cloves	remaining ingredients into
4	4	Cinnamon sticks, (4 inches, 10 cm, each in length), broken up	small cheesecloth bag. Put bag and juices into saucepan. Heat. Hold below boiling until spice flavor comes through. Makes 8 cups (2 L).

Grape Punch
A darker punch due to grape juice.
Combines well with lemonade.

1 L	**4 cups**	Purple grape juice	Combine grape juice,
½ × **341 mL**	½ × **12 oz.**	Frozen concentrated	concentrated lemonade
		lemonade, thawed	and water in punch bowl.
250 mL	**1 cup**	Water	Chill until needed.
1.5 L	**6 cups**	Tonic water or ginger ale	Add tonic water for a tart
			flavor or ginger ale for a
		Pictured below.	slightly sweeter flavor. Makes
			11½ cups (2.8 L).

Cranberry Punch, page 42   Grape Punch, page 43

Punch Bowls And Glasses Courtesy Of: Enchanted Kitchen, Le Gnome And Stokes

Spring Punch
Light orange colored. Combines orange, pineapple and cranberry flavors.

341 mL	12 oz.	Frozen concentrated orange juice, thawed	Pour first 4 ingredients into punch bowl. Chill until ready to serve.
1.5 L	6 cups	Prepared orange juice	
3 L	12 cups	Pineapple juice	
1.25 L	5 cups	Cranberry cocktail	
1.25 L	5 cups	Ginger ale	Add ginger ale. Stir gently.
		Thin orange slices	Add orange slices.
		Party Ice Ring, page 51	Add ice ring just before serving. Makes 32 cups (8 L).

Pictured below.

Punch Bowl Courtesy Of:
The Bay

Slushy Banana Punch

Banana and orange flavors team up to be a definite winner. An excellent slush.

1 L	4 cups	Hot water	Stir hot water and sugar together in large bowl to dissolve sugar.
650 mL	2⅔ cups	Granulated sugar	
1½ × 341 mL	1½ × 12 oz.	Frozen concentrated orange juice, thawed	Add next 4 ingredients. Stir. Divide into 2 containers. Freeze.
341 mL	12 oz.	Frozen concentrated lemonade, thawed	
1 L	4 cups	Pineapple juice	
4	4	Bananas, mashed or puréed	
2 × 2 L	2 × 2 qts.	Ginger ale or lemon-lime soft drink (such as 7-Up)	Put frozen chunk from 1 container into punch bowl. Add 2 quarts (2 L) ginger ale. Let stand for 20 minutes. Stir with a wire whisk to make slushy. Makes about 15 cups (3.75 L) or 30 cups (7.5 L) for whole recipe.

Mixed Citrus Punch

A fresh citrus flavor. Golden yellow with strawberries and mint leaves floating on top.

2 L	8 cups	Pineapple juice	Pour first 5 ingredients into punch bowl. Stir to dissolve sugar. Chill until ready to serve.
		Juice of 4 oranges	
		Juice of 4 lemons	
		Juice of 4 limes	
250 mL	1 cup	Granulated sugar	
2.5 L	10 cups	Ginger ale	Add ginger ale and club soda. Stir gently. Carefully add strawberries and mint leaves. To store leftover punch in refrigerator, remove mint leaves. Makes 24 cups (6 L).
1.25 L	5 cups	Club soda	
250 mL	1 cup	Fresh strawberries	
30 mL	2 tbsp.	Mint leaves	

Pictured on front cover.

ALCOHOL CITRUS PUNCH: For a 3 to 1 mix add 8 cups (2 L) vodka, gin or light rum. For a 4 to 1 mix add 6 cups (1.5 L) vodka, gin or light rum.

Amaretto Punch

An unusual punch. Amaretto flavor comes through well.

2 x 341 mL	2 x 12 oz.	Frozen concentrated orange juice, thawed	Pour first 3 ingredients into punch bowl. Stir.
2 L	8 cups	Club soda	
375 mL	1½ cups	Amaretto	
		Ice Ring of choice, page 51	Add ice ring. Makes 13 cups (3.25 L).

Lemon Tea Punch
Yellow and almost clear. Very cool looking. Just what's needed on a hot summer day.

2	2	Orange pekoe tea bags	Combine tea bags and
2 L	8 cups	Boiling water	boiling water in saucepan. Cover. Let steep for 10 minutes. Press liquid from bags.
250 mL	1 cup	Granulated sugar	Add sugar to hot tea. Stir to
250 mL	1 cup	Lemon juice, fresh is best (about 4 to 5 lemons), or bottled	dissolve. Add lemon juice. Pour into punch bowl. Chill in refrigerator.
1 L	4 cups	Ginger ale Ice cubes	Add ginger ale. Stir lightly. Serve over ice in glasses. Makes 14 cups (3.5 L).

Raspberry Fruit Punch
This makes a large batch of ruby-red punch.

3 L	3 qts.	Pineapple juice	Pour pineapple and
750 mL	3 cups	Grapefruit juice	grapefruit juice into punch
1 x 210 g	1 x 7½ oz.	Envelope raspberry drink crystals with sugar (about ½ cup, 125 mL)	bowl. Add raspberry drink crystals. Stir until dissolved. Refrigerate until ready to serve.
2 x 2 L	2 x 2 qts.	Ginger ale	Add ginger ale. Stir gently.
		Thin lemon and orange slices or Ice Ring of choice, page 51	Add fruit slices or ice ring. Makes 32 cups (8 L).

Percolator Punch

Pinky-orange. Reminiscent of a sunset.

1.1 L	4½ **cups**	Apple cider (or juice)
1.1 L	4½ **cups**	Prepared orange juice
1.1 L	4½ **cups**	Cranberry cocktail
30 mL	2 tbsp.	Lemon juice, fresh or bottled
0.5 mL	⅛ tsp.	Salt
175 mL	¾ **cup**	Brown sugar, packed
1	1	Cinnamon stick, (4 inches,10 cm, in length), broken up into slivers (see Note)
7 mL	1½ tsp.	Whole cloves
7 mL	1½ tsp.	Whole allspice

Give coffee percolator a thorough washing to remove any coffee traces. Pour first 5 ingredients into bottom part. Insert stem and basket.

Place sugar, cinnamon pieces, cloves and allspice in basket. Run through cycle. Makes 13½ cups (3 L).

Note: Put cinnamon stick into plastic bag. Break up with bottom of glass.

Pictured on page 49.

Punchy Tea

Refreshing pineapple with an aftertaste of raspberry and tea.

1 L	4 cups	Boiling water	Pour boiling water over tea bags in tea pot or saucepan. Cover. Steep for 10 minutes. Remove tea bags, pressing out liquid into tea pot.
2	2	Orange pekoe tea bags	
250 mL	1 cup	Granulated sugar	Stir sugar into hot tea until dissolved. Pour into punch bowl. Add pineapple and orange juice. Add raspberry crystals. Chill until ready to serve.
1.1 L	4½ cups	Pineapple juice	
1.1 L	4½ cups	Prepared orange juice	
60 mL	¼ cup	Raspberry flavored drink crystals	
1.1 L	4½ cups	Club soda	Add club soda. Stir lightly. Add ice ring or thin slices of orange. Makes 18½ cups (4.6 L).
		Ice Ring of choice, page 51	

Pictured below.

Percolator Punch, page 48   Punchy Tea, page 49

Glass Mugs Courtesy Of: The Bay

Garden Punch

Not only served in the garden. Great for Christmas parties and meetings. So easy.

1.5 L	6 cups	Pineapple juice	Mix first 3 ingredients in
½ × 341 mL	½ × 12 oz.	Frozen concentrated orange juice, thawed	punch bowl. Chill until needed.
30 mL	2 tbsp.	Lemon juice, fresh or bottled	
2 L	8 cups	Ginger ale Ice Ring of choice, page 51	Add ginger ale. Stir gently. Add ice ring. Makes 15 cups (3.75 L).

Strawberry Punch

This combo is a wonderful mixture. Very pretty.

425 g	15 oz.	Frozen sliced strawberries in syrup, thawed	Run strawberries and syrup through blender to smooth. Pour into punch bowl.
500 mL	2 cups	Pineapple juice	Add pineapple, orange and apple juice. Stir.
750 mL	3 cups	Orange juice	
250 mL	1 cup	Apple juice	
1 L	4 cups	Club soda or lemon-lime soft drink (such as 7-Up), (see Note)	Gently stir in club soda or lemon-lime soft drink just before serving. Makes 12 cups (3 L).

Note: Adding club soda makes punch slightly more tart. Adding lemon-lime soft drink makes punch a bit sweeter.

Ice Rings

Here are some simple ideas to create stunning ice rings!

MOLDS: Any round jelly mold or bowl is suitable for an ice ring. The shape of mold will determine what type of decorations or design you can make. Determine amount of liquid you need by filling mold with water then measuring amount used. To remove frozen ice ring, run cold water over bottom. Place bottom side up in punch.

PARTY ICE RING: Fill ring mold with sugar-free ginger ale. Ice melts too fast if it contains sugar. Cherries, strawberries or grapes may be added. Freeze. Unmold. Place fruit side up in punch bowl.
Pictured on page 44.

GRAPE & CANTALOUPE ICE RING: Pour diet lemon-lime soft drink (such as 7-Up) into desired mold to about ¹/₂ inch (12 mm) in depth. Freeze. Place mint leaves here and there on frozen drink. Arrange whole red seedless grapes and cantaloupe balls around leaves. Slowly pour more drink over fruit to cover about halfway. Freeze. Pour remaining drink to fill mold. Freeze.
Pictured on this page.

FRUITED ICE RING: Tint required amount of water with choice of food coloring. Arrange strawberry halves, cut side up, in bottom of desired mold. Add other pieces of fruit of choice around strawberries. Pour tinted water over fruit to ¹/₂ inch (12 mm) in depth. Freeze. Add another layer of tinted water to ¹/₄ inch (6 mm) in depth. Freeze. Pour remaining water to fill mold. Freeze.

PUNCH ICE RING: Make ice ring from punch. It won't dilute punch.

ICED TEA CUBES: Make ice cubes using tea so ice won't dilute tea drinks.

COFFEE ICE CUBES: Make ice cubes using coffee so ice won't dilute coffee drinks.

Punch Bowl Courtesy Of: K-Mart

Pink Lady Punch   *A pretty color and fruity flavor.*

1 L	4 cups	Cranberry cocktail	Mix first 3 ingredients. Chill if
1 L	4 cups	Pineapple juice	not using right away.
30 mL	2 tbsp.	Lemon juice, fresh or bottled	
2 L	9 cups	Ginger ale	Before serving, add ginger
		Lemon slices, paper thin	ale. Float lemon slices on

Before serving, add ginger ale. Float lemon slices on top. Score peel before slicing for a decorative look. Makes 17 cups (4.25 L).

PINK LADY WITH A PUNCH:
For a 3 to 1 mix add 5⅔ cups (1.4 L) vodka or gin. For a 4 to1 mix add 4¼ cups (1 L) vodka or gin.

Fruit Punch   *A good thirst quencher.*

1 L	4 cups	Prepared orange juice	Have all ingredients chilled.
500 mL	2 cups	Unsweetened pineapple juice	Combine orange, pineapple and lemon juice in pitcher.
15 mL	1 tbsp.	Lemon juice, fresh or bottled	Add soft drink. Stir lightly.
1 L	4 cups	Lemon-lime soft drink (such as 7-Up)	Ginger ale may be used instead of lemon-lime soft drink but the color will be

Ginger ale may be used instead of lemon-lime soft drink but the color will be dull rather than bright. Makes 10 cups (2.5 L).

Party Punch
Light colored and flavorful.

½ × 341 mL	½ × 12 oz.	Frozen concentrated orange juice, thawed
½ × 341 mL	½ × 12 oz.	Frozen concentrated lemonade, thawed
675 mL	3 cups	Pineapple juice, chilled
1 L	4½ cups	Water
675 mL	3 cups	Ginger ale, chilled

Pour all ingredients into punch bowl. If not serving right away, add ginger ale later. Stir gently. Add ice ring of choice. Makes 12 cups (2.7 L).

PINEAPPLE ICE RING:
Arrange pineapple rings in bottom of desired mold. Place whole maraschino cherry in center of each ring. In separate container, measure ½ pineapple juice and ½ water. Stir. Slowly pour over fruit to about ⅛ inch (3 mm) deep. Freeze. Add more pineapple-water mixture to just cover fruit. Freeze. Pour remaining mixture to fill mold. Freeze.

Pictured below.

Pictured on this page.

Fruit Shake

Try all three variations of cantaloupe, papaya and mango. A very thick shake.

250 mL	1 cup	Strawberry non-fat yogurt
250 mL	1 cup	Cut up cantaloupe, papaya or mango
250 mL	1 cup	Frozen whole strawberries, coarsely chopped
		Granulated sugar, to taste (optional)

Add all ingredients to blender. Process until smooth. The fruit in order of thickest shake is papaya, then mango, then cantaloupe making the least thick. Makes 2 cups (500 mL).

Cherry Shake

A thick creamy texture. Dark cherry color.

250 mL	1 cup	Plain yogurt
250 mL	1 cup	Frozen pitted Bing cherries or fresh, pitted
15 mL	1 tbsp.	Granulated sugar
1 mL	¼ tsp.	Almond flavoring (or use 1 tsp., 5 mL, vanilla)

Combine all ingredients in blender. Process until blended. Makes 2 cups (500 mL). Serves 1.

Pictured on page 55.

1. **Cherry Shake, page 54**
2. **Breakfast Shake, page 57**
3. **Choco Breakfast Shake, page 57**

Eye Opener

Garnish with a wedge of fresh pineapple and serve with a straw.

250 mL	1 cup	Pineapple juice
1	1	Large egg, raw
15 mL	1 tbsp.	Brown sugar
75 mL	⅓ cup	Skim milk powder
60 mL	¼ cup	Crushed ice

Pictured below.

Purée all ingredients in blender. Process until smooth. Makes 1½ cups (375 mL).

GRAPEFRUIT EYE OPENER:
Use grapefruit juice in place of pineapple. Since this is so tart, add more sugar to taste.

Glassware Courtesy Of: Stokes

Breakfast Shake

The wheat germ disappears into this shake.

250 mL	1 cup	Strawberry yogurt	Put all ingredients into
125 mL	½ cup	Prepared orange juice	blender. Process until
1	1	Medium banana, cut up	smooth. Makes 2 cups
15 mL	1 tbsp.	Wheat germ (optional)	(500 mL). Serves 1.

BLUEBERRY BREAKFAST SHAKE: Use blueberry yogurt.

PEACH BREAKFAST SHAKE: Use peach yogurt.

RASPBERRY BREAKFAST SHAKE: Use raspberry yogurt.

Note: Use non-fat or low-fat yogurt for a diet shake. Use only ½ banana if you want more yogurt flavor. Using 1 banana makes shake thicker.

Pictured on page 55.

Choco Breakfast Shake

Get your protein on the run. Tastes like chocolate milk.

250 mL	1 cup	Milk	Put all ingredients in the
1	1	Large egg, raw	blender. Process until smooth
30 mL	2 tbsp.	Sweetened hot chocolate mix	and frothy. Makes 1½ cups (375 mL).
0.5 mL	⅛ tsp.	Vanilla	

Pictured on page 55.

Apricot Drink

Coral color with orange flecks. Thick and foamy.

250 mL	1 cup	Milk	Process all ingredients in
4	4	Large ripe apricots, halved and pitted	blender until smooth. Apricots in season won't require much sweetening if any.
5 mL	1 tsp.	Vanilla	Apricots out of season may
		Granulated sugar, to taste	require up to 2 tbsp. (30 mL)

Pictured on page 63.

Apricots out of season may require up to 2 tbsp. (30 mL) sugar. Makes 2 cups (500 mL).

Tea Soda

Hot sweetened tea and ice cream makes a very different dessert or snack.

1.1 L	4½ cups	Boiling water	Pour boiling water over tea bags in tea pot. Cover. Let steep for 10 minutes.
3	3	Orange pekoe tea bags	
125 mL	½ cup	Corn syrup	Stir in corn syrup. Pour hot mixture into soda glasses until ½ full, about ¾ cup (175 mL).
		Vanilla ice cream	Top with rounded scoop of ice cream. Fill with club soda. Makes 5 cups (1.25 L) hot mixture for about 6 sodas.
		Club soda or lemon-lime soft drink (such as 7-Up)	

Pictured on page 59.

Tropical Blend

All your favorites from the tropics with natural sweetness. Nice and thick.

Metric	Imperial	Ingredient
250 mL	1 cup	Crushed pineapple with juice
1	1	Medium banana, cut up
125 mL	½ cup	Prepared orange juice
15 mL	1 tbsp.	Medium coconut
5 mL	1 tsp.	Lemon juice, fresh or bottled
15 mL	1 tbsp.	Wheat germ (optional)

Put everything into blender. Process until blended. Serve immediately. Makes 2 cups (500 mL).

Pictured below.

1

2

1. Tea Soda, page 58
2. Tropical Blend, page 59

Glassware Courtesy Of: Le Gnome

Veggie Shake

*Supplies juice, vegetable and protein.
Looks a bit like tomato soup.*

250 mL	1 cup	Tomato juice	Measure all 8 ingredients
128 mL	4½ oz.	Strained carrots (baby food)	into blender. Process until smooth. Makes 1½ cups
1	1	Large egg, raw or hard boiled	(375 mL).
125 mL	½ cup	Plain or vanilla yogurt	**Pictured on page 63.**
10 mL	2 tsp.	Lemon juice, fresh or bottled	
1 mL	¼ tsp.	Onion powder	
1 mL	¼ tsp.	Worcestershire sauce	
1 mL	¼ tsp.	Salt	

Peach Whirl

*Always a welcome flavor. Try with and without
almond flavoring. Frothy and thick.*

500 mL	2 cups	Peach yogurt	Purée yogurt and peaches
398 mL	14 oz.	Canned peaches with juice	with juice in blender. Add almond flavoring. Process
2 mL	½ tsp.	Almond flavoring, scant measure (optional)	until smooth.
250 mL	1 cup	Crushed ice (about 5 cubes)	Put crushed ice into tall glasses. Pour blender contents over top. Makes 4 cups (1 L).

Variation: Add crushed ice to first 3 ingredients in blender. Process.

Blueberry Shake
A good berry shake with yogurt and an egg.

125 mL	½ cup	Blueberry yogurt
125 mL	½ cup	Blueberries, fresh or frozen
1	1	Large egg, raw (see Note)
15 mL	1 tbsp.	Granulated sugar
1 mL	¼ tsp.	Vanilla

Pictured on front cover.

Measure all ingredients into blender. Process until blended. Taste for sweetness, adding a bit more sugar if desired. Makes a scant 1 cup (250 mL).

Note: A hard-boiled egg may be used rather than raw. Purée egg with yogurt then add blueberries, sugar and vanilla and process. Flavor of egg is not noticeable. A bit thicker shake when using a hard-boiled egg. Makes a scant 1 cup (250 mL).

Smoothie
Fruit juice and yogurt makes for a great quick breakfast.

140 g	5 oz.	Vanilla yogurt
1	1	Banana, cut up
125 mL	½ cup	Apple juice
5 mL	1 tsp.	Granulated sugar (optional)
300 mL	1¼ cups	Crushed ice (about 6 large cubes)

Measure all ingredients into blender. Process until smooth. Makes 2 cups (500 mL).

Malted Shake

More frozen yogurt may be added to this if desired. Try all the variations too. Wonderful with fresh strawberries.

250 mL	1 cup	Milk
50 mL	3 tbsp.	Malted milk powder (such as Ovaltine)
125 mL	½ cup	Frozen vanilla yogurt

Process all 3 ingredients in blender until smooth. Makes 2 cups (500 mL).

STRAWBERRY MALT: Add 3 to 4 fresh strawberries for a pretty pink color or add 1 tbsp. (15 mL) strawberry jam for a creamy white color.

STRAWBERRY YOGURT MALT: Omit frozen yogurt. Add same amount of vanilla or strawberry yogurt. Add 3 to 4 fresh strawberries or 1 tbsp. (15 mL) strawberry jam.

CHOCOLATE MALTED SHAKE: Omit malted milk powder. Add same amount of chocolate malted milk powder.

MALTED YOGURT DRINK: Omit frozen yogurt. Add same amount of vanilla yogurt.

Black Currant Shake

A smooth thick shake in a pretty mauve shade. Start your day with color.

250 mL	**1 cup**	Plain yogurt, no fat or regular	Place yogurt, banana and jelly in blender. Process until smooth. Makes 1¾ cups (425 mL).
½	½	Medium banana, cut up	
60 mL	**¼ cup**	Black currant jelly preserves	

Pictured below.

Black Currant Shake, page 63   Apricot Drink, page 58   Veggie Shake, page 60

Blender And Glasses Courtesy Of: Eaton's

Frozen Fruit Slush

Pretty with or without grenadine.
Keep on hand in your freezer.

Fruit Slush

750 mL	3 cups	Granulated sugar	Boil sugar and water slowly
1.5 L	6 cups	Water	in saucepan for 5 minutes.
			Cool. Pour into ice cream
			pail.
1.5 L	6 cups	Pineapple juice	Add next 5 ingredients. Mix
		Juice of 5 oranges	well. Freeze. Makes 24 cups
		Juice of 2 lemons	(6 L).
5	5	Medium bananas, mashed	
		until smooth	
250 mL	1 cup	Gin	

To Serve

150 mL	⅔ cup	Frozen slush, above	Measure all 4 ingredients into
45 mL	1½ oz.	Gin	tall glass. Stir gently. Serves 1.
150 mL	⅔ cup	Ginger ale (more if desired)	
5 mL	1 tsp.	Grenadine (optional but	
		pretty)	

Summer Slush

When company comes on hot summer days, there's no worries with this large recipe in the freezer.

1.5 L	6 cups	Water	Divide the first 5 ingredients
341 mL	12 oz.	Frozen concentrated orange juice, thawed	evenly between 2 ice cream pails. Stir well.
341 mL	12 oz.	Frozen concentrated lemonade, thawed	
1.5 L	6 cups	Pineapple juice	
1.5 L	6 cups	Prepared orange juice	
4	4	Medium bananas, cut up	Process bananas and
425 g	15 oz.	Frozen sliced strawberries in syrup, thawed	strawberries with syrup in blender. Divide evenly
750 mL	26 oz.	Vodka, gin or white rum	between pails. Stir. Add 1/2 vodka to each pail. Stir. Cover and freeze.

To Serve

Lemon-lime soft drink (such as 7-Up) or cream soda

Fill glass 1/2 full with frozen mixture. Fill with lemon-lime soft drink for a golden slush. Fill with cream soda for a pink slush. Makes 27 cups (6.75 L) of slush.

Slushy Punch

Fruity banana flavor. Most refreshing.

Slush

500 mL	2 cups	Granulated sugar
3	3	Bananas, cut up
750 mL	3 cups	Water

Add sugar, banana and water to blender. Process until smooth. Pour into ice cream pail.

341 mL	12 oz.	Frozen concentrated orange juice, thawed
½ × 341 mL	½ × 12 oz.	Frozen concentrated lemonade, thawed
750 mL	3 cups	Pineapple juice

Add orange juice, lemonade and pineapple juice. Stir. Divide and freeze ½ in each of 2 containers. Makes 9²/₃ cups (2.4 L) Slush.

To Serve

3 L	3 qts.	Ginger ale

Let Slush thaw for 2 hours on counter. Add 6 cups (1.5 L) ginger ale to each container. Serve while slushy. Makes 22 cups (5.5 L) punch.

Pictured on this page.

Glassware Courtesy Of: Enchanted Kitchen

Peach Slush
Made from canned peaches, this recipe makes a small quantity.

398 mL	14 oz.	Canned sliced peaches with juice	Combine peaches with juice, sugar and lemon juice in blender. Process until smooth. Pour into ungreased 9 x 9 inch (22 x 22 cm) pan. Freeze.
75 mL	1/3 cup	Granulated sugar	
15 mL	1 tbsp.	Lemon juice, fresh or bottled	
		Ginger ale	Scoop into tall glass a scant 1/2 full of slush. Add ginger ale to fill glass. Makes 2¹/₄ cups (560 mL) slush, enough to make 3 large glasses.

Cranberry Slush
You may want to double this for your punch bowl. A creamy raspberry flavor. Really good.

1 L	4 cups	Cranberry cocktail	Mix first 3 ingredients in medium container. Freeze.
1/2 × 341 mL	1/2 × 12 oz.	Frozen concentrated orange juice, thawed	
1/2 × 341 mL	1/2 × 12 oz.	Frozen concentrated lemonade, thawed	
1 L	4 cups	Ginger ale	Turn frozen mixture into punch bowl. Add ginger ale. Stir. Spoon in sherbet. Makes 12 cups (3 L).
500 mL	2 cups	Raspberry sherbet	

Pictured on page 69.

Brandy Slush

This will be a favorite after the first try. Apricot color.

1.75 L	7 cups	Water	Boil water and sugar in saucepan for 1 minute. Remove from heat. Pour into ice cream pail.
250 mL	1 cup	Granulated sugar	
500 mL	2 cups	Boiling water	Pour boiling water over tea bags in teapot. Let steep for 10 minutes. Remove tea bags, pressing out liquid. Add tea to pail. Stir.
4	4	Orange pekoe tea bags	
341 mL	12 oz.	Frozen concentrated lemonade, partially thawed	Add lemonade, orange juice and brandy. Stir. Freeze.
341 mL	12 oz.	Frozen concentrated orange juice, partially thawed	
500 mL	2 cups	Peach or apricot brandy	
		Ginger ale, to fill	Fill tall glass ⅔ full of slush. Add ginger ale. Serve with a straw if desired. Makes 14½ cups (3.5 L).

Pictured on page 69.

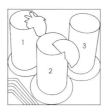

1. **Slushy Fruit Cooler, page 70**
2. **Brandy Slush, page 68**
3. **Cranberry Slush, page 67**

Glassware Courtesy Of: Le Gnome And Zeller's

Slushy Fruit Cooler

Strictly a fruit slush for a hot day.

750 mL	3 cups	Hot water	Stir hot water and sugar
250 mL	1 cup	Granulated sugar	together in ice cream pail to dissolve sugar.
1 L	4 cups	Unsweetened grapefruit juice	Add next 4 ingredients. Stir.
1 L	4 cups	Pineapple juice	
341 mL	12 oz.	Frozen concentrated orange juice	
341 mL	12 oz.	Frozen concentrated lemonade	
600 g	21 oz.	Frozen whole strawberries, cut up	Purée strawberries, citric acid and second amount
4 mL	¾ tsp.	Citric Acid (drug store)	of water in blender. You will
1 L	4 cups	Water	need to do it in 2 batches. Add to pail. Stir. Freeze.
		Tonic water	Combine about 2 parts slush with 1 part tonic water in tall
		Pictured on page 69.	glass. Makes 9 cups (2.25 L) slush.

Alcohol Variation: Gin or vodka may be added if desired.

Apple Spiced Tea

A clear rosy color. Serve in glass mugs for a pretty drink on a cold night. Easy to increase.

1.1 L	4½ cups	Apple juice	Heat apple juice, crushed
1	1	Cinnamon stick, (4 inches, 10 cm, in length), broken up and crushed in plastic bag	cinnamon, cloves and sugar in saucepan. Stir often until boiling. Remove from heat.
5	5	Whole cloves	
5 mL	1 tsp.	Granulated sugar	
2	2	Orange pekoe tea bags	Add tea bags. Cover. Steep for 5 minutes. Makes 4¼ cups (1 L).

Pictured on page 73.

Rummy Tea

Although adding a sweetener is optional, it tends to bring out all the flavors.

45 mL	1½ oz.	Light rum (or gold)	Put rum, lemon juice and
2 mL	½ tsp.	Lemon juice, fresh or bottled	lemon twist into mug. Add tea to fill.
1	1	Lemon twist	
		Hot orange pekoe tea to fill mug	
15 mL	1 tbsp.	Sugar Syrup, page 12, or to taste	Add Sugar Syrup. Stir.

Dessert Tea

A heartwarming and soothing drink. Good to serve with or without dessert.

15 mL	½ oz.	Grand Marnier	Measure Grand Marnier and
15 mL	½ oz.	Amaretto	Amaretto into an 8 oz.
		Hot orange pekoe tea	(250 mL) mug. Fill with tea.

Whipped cream or topping, to cover
Grated chocolate or cinnamon, sprinkle (optional)

Top with whipped cream. Sprinkle with chocolate or cinnamon. Makes 1 serving.

Pictured on front cover.

Tea Treat

Amber colored tea with great additions. Very good.

1.5 L	6 cups	Water	Measure first amount of
1	1	Orange pekoe tea bag (or 1 tbsp., 15 mL loose tea)	water into saucepan. Add tea and sugar. Heat, stirring often until it comes to a boil.
300 mL	1¼ cups	Granulated sugar (can use less)	Boil slowly for 1 minute. Cover. Remove from heat. Let stand for 10 minutes.

Juice of 3 lemons
Juice of 3 oranges

Add lemon juice and orange juice. Strain to remove pulp. If you used less sugar, taste. Stir in more if desired.

Ice cubes or crushed ice

Serve over ice in tall glasses. Makes 13½ cups (3.37 L).

Blueberry Tea

Serve in your best tea cups after a special meal.

30 mL	1 oz.	Grand Marnier	Measure Grand Marnier into

Hot orange pekoe tea — Measure Grand Marnier into tea cup. Fill with hot tea. Makes 1 serving.

Pictured on this page.

Tea Tip

Tea leaves are graded and sorted by size (larger, coarser leaves taking a longer time to brew). Orange pekoe is often mistaken for the flavor of a tea when, in fact, pekoe describes a medium size, slightly coarser tea leaf. Orange pekoe refers to the smallest and youngest leaf of the plant.

1. Blueberry Tea, page 73
2. Apple Spiced Tea, page 71

Sun Tea

This tea is steeped all day in cold water in the sun.
It even works steeped on the kitchen counter. Give it a try.

4 L	16 cups	Water	Pour water into 1 gallon (4 L)
5	5	Orange pekoe tea bags	jar. Add tea bags. Cover.
			Let stand in sunlight all day.
			Remove tea bags, pressing
			out liquid. Transfer tea to a
			larger container.
125 mL	½ cup	Granulated sugar	Add sugar and concentrated
341 mL	12 oz.	Frozen concentrated	lemonade. Stir until sugar
		lemonade, thawed	dissolves. Makes 18 cups
			(4.5 L).

Iced Tea

Cold tea method. Steeps in refrigerator. No fuss, no mess.

4 L	1 gal.	Cold water	Pour water over tea bags in
16-19	16-19	Orange pekoe tea bags	1 gallon (4 L) jar. Cover.
			Refrigerate for 24 hours.
			Resist the urge to sample
			before 24 hours have
			passed.
		Ice cubes	Pour over ice cubes in tall
		Sugar Syrup, page 12	glasses. Sweeten to taste
			with Sugar Syrup. Makes 1
		Pictured on front cover.	gallon (4 L).

Measurement Tables

Throughout this book measurements are given in Conventional and Metric measure. To compensate for differences between the two measurements due to rounding, a full metric measure is not always used. The cup used is the standard 8 fluid ounce. Temperature is given in degrees Fahrenheit and Celsius. Baking pan measurements are in inches and centimetres. An exact metric conversion is given below as well as the working equivalent (Standard Measure).

SPOONS

Conventional Measure	Metric Exact Conversion Millilitre (mL)	Metric Standard Measure Millilitre (mL)
1/8 teaspoon (tsp.)	0.6 mL	0.5 mL
1/4 teaspoon (tsp.)	1.2 mL	1 mL
1/2 teaspoon (tsp.)	2.4 mL	2 mL
1 teaspoon (tsp.)	4.7 mL	5 mL
2 teaspoons (tsp.)	9.4 mL	10 mL
1 tablespoon (tbsp.)	14.2 mL	15 mL

CUPS

1/4 cup (4 tbsp.)	56.8 mL	60 mL
1/3 cup (5 1/3 tbsp.)	75.6 mL	75 mL
1/2 cup (8 tbsp.)	113.7 mL	125 mL
2/3 cup (10 2/3 tbsp.)	151.2 mL	150 mL
3/4 cup (12 tbsp.)	170.5 mL	175 mL
1 cup (16 tbsp.)	227.3 mL	250 mL
4 1/2 cups	1022.9 mL	1000 mL (1 L)

CASSEROLES (Canada & Britain)

Standard Size Casserole	Exact Metric Measure
1 qt. (5 cups)	1.13 L
1 1/2 qts. (7 1/2 cups)	1.69 L
2 qts. (10 cups)	2.25 L
2 1/2 qts. (12 1/2 cups)	2.81 L
3 qts. (15 cups)	3.38 L
4 qts. (20 cups)	4.5 L
5 qts. (25 cups)	5.63 L

CASSEROLES (United States)

Standard Size Casserole	Exact Metric Measure
1 qt. (4 cups)	900 mL
1 1/2 qts. (6 cups)	1.35 L
2 qts. (8 cups)	1.8 L
2 1/2 qts. (10 cups)	2.25 L
3 qts. (12 cups)	2.7 L
4 qts. (16 cups)	3.6 L
5 qts. (20 cups)	4.5 L

DRY MEASUREMENTS

Conventional Measure Ounces (oz.)	Exact Conversion Grams (g)	Standard Measure Grams (g)
1 oz.	28.3 g	30 g
2 oz.	56.7 g	55 g
3 oz.	85.0 g	85 g
4 oz.	113.4 g	125 g
5 oz.	141.7 g	140 g
6 oz.	170.1 g	170 g
7 oz.	198.4 g	200 g
8 oz.	226.8 g	250 g
16 oz.	453.6 g	500 g
32 oz.	907.2 g	1000 g (1 kg)

PANS

Conventional Inches	Metric Centimetres
8x8 inch	20x20 cm
9x9 inch	22x22 cm
9x13 inch	22x33 cm
10x15 inch	25x38 cm
11x17 inch	28x43 cm
8x2 inch round	20x5 cm
9x2 inch round	22x5 cm
10x4 1/2 inch tube	25x11 cm
8x4x3 inch loaf	20x10x7 cm
9x5x3 inch loaf	22x12x7 cm

OVEN TEMPERATURES

Fahrenheit (°F)	Celsius (°C)
175°	80°
200°	95°
225°	110°
250°	120°
275°	140°
300°	150°
325°	160°
350°	175°
375°	190°
400°	205°
425°	220°
450°	230°
475°	240°
500°	260°

Index

MAIL ORDER FORM

Deduct $5.00 for every $35.00 ordered

Save $5.00

COMPANY'S COMING SERIES

Quantity		Quantity		Quantity	
	150 Delicious Squares		Vegetables		Microwave Cooking
	Casseroles		Main Courses		Preserves
	Muffins & More		Pasta		Light Casseroles
	Salads		Cakes		Chicken, Etc.
	Appetizers		Barbecues		Kids Cooking
	Desserts		Dinners of the World		Fish & Seafood
	Soups & Sandwiches		Lunches		Breads
	Holiday Entertaining		Pies		Meatless Cooking
	Cookies		Light Recipes		Cooking For Two

NO. OF BOOKS | **PRICE**

FIRST BOOK: $12.99 + $3.00 shipping = **$15.99 each** x _____ = $ _____

ADDITIONAL BOOKS: $12.99 + $1.50 shipping = **$14.49 each** x _____ = $ _____

PINT SIZE BOOKS

Quantity		Quantity		Quantity	
	Finger Food		Buffets		Chocolate
	Party Planning		Baking Delights		Beverages

NO. OF BOOKS | **PRICE**

FIRST BOOK: $4.99 + $2.00 shipping = **$6.99 each** x _____ = $ _____

ADDITIONAL BOOKS: $4.99 + $1.00 shipping = **$5.99 each** x _____ = $ _____

- **MAKE CHEQUE OR MONEY ORDER PAYABLE TO:** *COMPANY'S COMING PUBLISHING LIMITED*

- **ORDERS OUTSIDE CANADA:** *Must be paid in U.S. funds by cheque or money order drawn on Canadian or U.S. bank.*

- *Prices subject to change without prior notice.*

- *Sorry, no C.O.D.'s*

TOTAL PRICE FOR ALL BOOKS	$
Less $5.00 for every $35.00 ordered —	$
SUBTOTAL	$
Canadian residents add G.S.T./H.S.T. +	$
TOTAL AMOUNT ENCLOSED	$

Please complete shipping address on reverse.

Gift Giving

- Let us help you with your gift giving!
- We will send cookbooks directly to the recipients of your choice if you give us their names and addresses.
- Be sure to specify the titles you wish to send to each person.
- If you would like to include your personal note or card, we will be pleased to enclose it with your gift order.
- Company's Coming Cookbooks make excellent gifts. Birthdays, bridal showers, Mother's Day, Father's Day, graduation or any occasion... collect them all!

Shipping address

Send the Company's Coming Cookbooks listed on the reverse side of this coupon, to:

Name:

Street:

City: Province/State:

Postal Code/Zip: Tel: ( ) —

Company's Coming Publishing Limited
Box 8037, Station F
Edmonton, Alberta, Canada T6H 4N9
Tel: (403) 450-6223
Fax: (403) 450-1857